MW01519151

# *Grip the Doorknob*

## *(Mostly Funny Poems)*

# *Grip the Doorknob*

## *(Mostly Funny Poems)*

*by*

**Marcia Taylor**

Dear Gwen -
Hope you find something
funny in here!
Marcia
May 2019

Copyright © April 2019 by Marcia Taylor

First printing, 2019
Printed in the United States of America

ISBN: 978-1-9995368-0-0

Available from Amazon.com and other on-line and retail outlets

For additional information, please contact
gripthedoorknob@gmail.com

*To my great-great-grandfather,*
*William Porter,*
*who wrote and published a book*
*of elaborate religious poetry in 1892,*
*and confidently sent a copy off to Queen Victoria.*

*There's something very authentic about humor, when you think about it. Anybody can pretend to be serious. But you can't pretend to be funny.*

*Billy Collins, Poet Laureate of the United States, 2001-2003*

# Contents

where did this? come from

✓

# Grip the Doorknob

### *(Mostly Funny Poems)*

## *Aging Gracefully*

Start the day with probiotics,
Don my woolen underwear,
Prop me up on good orthotics,
Fetch my glasses, all three pair.

Load my purse with medication,
Diuretics and green tea,
Set my cell phone on vibration,
Print a google map for me.

Where's my Purell? Get my Splenda.
Find the grippers for my feet.
Don't forget the comfy slippers,
Obus form and heated seat.

Thursday is the Shoppers discount,
Wednesday brings the CPP.
Tuesday, movie and line dancing,
Monday, my bone density.

Sign me up for finger painting,

Put my mittens on a string.

Friday, it's Casino Rama!

Oh, the fun old age can bring.

## *All Hallows' Eve*

Under the spell of the bright gibbous moon,
Skeletons conjure a bone rattling tune,
And witches on switches sweep over the heath,
Hexing and cursing all poor souls beneath.

Ashes hide faces, and candle light flickers
On wandering bands of disguised treat or tricksters.
Bonfires roar skyward, the smoke purifying,
Now zombies are risen, their cries terrifying.

Ghouls in the shadows who whisper, "Hallooo,"
Old vampires and bats join the spook retinue.
Incantations and spells cannot banish the dread,
As tonight by the moon, we must host the undead.

Take up a lantern, but shroud all your features,
And roam through the land with the moaners and screechers.
Superstition and magic, for those who believe,
Say — prepare for a haunting this All Hallows' Eve!

## *And Little Pink Piggies Can Fly*

Pesticides help feed the planet,
Protecting our crops from disease,
But our corn is refined into ethanol gas,
Putting cars before people, and bees.

Olympic Committees are moral,
They choose their host countries with care,
Though they don't run or jump, or take physical risk,
They outscore the best athletes there.

Reporters are now entertainers,
Writing stories instead of the facts.
They throw in some gossip, or hearsay, or lies,
And then watch how the country reacts.

The media speak only truth they say,
And senators, they never lie,
Olympians show us the best of the best,
And little pink piggies can fly, can fly,
And little pink piggies can fly.

## *Autistic*

*A Villanelle poem has 19 lines consisting of five tercets and a quatrain, with a particular rhyme scheme. This Villanelle was inspired by singer Paul Reddick's song, "Villanelle."*

Where others see the darkness, you see light,
And count the minutes, while I rant and wail.
For you there is no sorrow, blame, or fright.

You pace until the day eclipses night,
Your eyes too bright, your skin so taut and pale,
Where others see the darkness, you see light.

I turn away, and leave you to your fight.
Some moments I recall, though through a veil
For you there is no sorrow, blame, or fright.

You fly, not like a bird, but like a kite,
Your life is held in orbit, not a jail.
Where others see the darkness, you see light.

Accepting life as neither wrong, nor right
When daily struggles leave your body frail,
For you there is no sorrow, blame, or fright.

Your fiery charms no longer thought a blight,
With open-hearted friendship you prevail.
All those who tried to change you, now contrite.
Where once was only darkness, now is light.

## *Autumn I*

*Written when I was in Grade Five.*

Leaves are falling to the ground,
Red and yellow, orange and brown,
And the fairies love this sight,
For they dance in the leaves at night.

The moon comes out, the sun goes in,
See the fairies dance and spin.
Now the fall is here at last,
But the summer went too fast.

## Autumn is the Glory Time

*Inspired by the line, "Autumn's the mellow time" by poet William Allingham.*

Autumn is the glory time,
When the burning bush ignites,
And the maples cast a peachy glow over the kitchen,
When the red oak dons a new coat of brown leather,
And the low sun sets fire to tree tops,
And warms the pumpkins waiting patiently in the field.

Autumn is the bridging time,
When sun and snow reconcile,
An interlude, tied by misty dawn and glimmering dusk,
The rich time between ripening and rot,
When deer assemble along the lane,
And hornets dance on warm brick, looking for a way in.

Autumn is the dying time,
When darkness overtakes, and urges are dulled.
The elderberry shrivels and shrinks, drying weeds rattle,
Flowers nod, and grasses bow to a waning sun.
Blackbirds gather on the wire to watch frantic geese,
And spongy leaves blanket the white grub, which sleeps.

## *Best Perennials*

*Nonet, a nine-line poem, with nine syllables in the first line, eight in the second, and so on.*

Best perennials for cut flowers
Peony, monkshood, lupin, phlox
Fleabane, liatris, yarrow
Lily of the valley
Sneezeweed and daisy
Delphinium
Bellflower
Tickseed
Sage

*To Betty Brown, on the occasion of her 90<sup>th</sup> birthday*

If you see a frown on Betty Brown,
Undoubtedly, you're upside down.

## Biker Rules of the Road

*Written after sitting in traffic behind an aging biker.*

A biker needs a strong name that's hard and tough and manly,
Like Scar, or Scab, or Blackjack, not Jim, or Ted, or Stanley.

The biker is an outlaw, we don't care to get along,
We roar around the countryside and look for rights to wrong.

We growl and snarl and scratch ourselves and never crack a smile,
And when we get our "hogs" revved up you'll hear 'em for a mile.

Here's the Nazi helmet that I wear when I am datin',
And I got a sidecar for my pit bull, name of Satan.

My biker boots are rhino skin with laces to the knees,
These spikes around my neck can open cans of beans with ease.

Got biker gloves with fringes and a sleeveless black T-shirt,
The skull and crossbones logo tells the world to eat my dirt.

My grungy leather vest with holes is from the discount store,
For clothes already shot at, you must pay a little more.

These shiny motorcycle pants fit like a second skin,
They cut down wind resistance and they hold my belly in.
Don't try to steal my wallet 'cause it's on a six-foot chain,
I shortened it in case I snag a parking sign again.

The freedom of the open road, the warrior's refrain,
Another bug between my teeth and I will go insane.

But it's hard to keep my image up like Hecate, or Rasputin,
When the "tat" upon my chest proclaims...
    "INTOLERANCE TO GLUTEN."

***But not today…***

I want to say your name to strangers,
I want to tell how it all happened,
Someday,
Maybe tomorrow,
But not today.

I want to see your crooked smile,
I want to look at our photographs and laugh,
Someday,
Maybe tomorrow,
But not today.

I want to write your story,
I want to explain how you endured,
Someday,
Maybe tomorrow,
But not today.

## *Chaos*

*Psychologist Jordan Peterson says we should rid our lives of chaos, and get our own houses in order.*

Oh, I have lived in chaos,
It's such a heady place,
The shocking unexpected times,
The learning curve's embrace.

Productive in the darkness,
Then wilting in the day,
Overflowing grand ideas
Suck my energy away.

But, my chaos now is ordered,
My life a single path,
Tonight I scrub the kitchen floor,
Tomorrow night, I bath.

## Cousin Cosmo

There was a special birthday
Back in June of '42,
So, we checked the funny papers
And it turns out it was you.

Westley Murdoch Thornton
Was a name that had some flow,
But instead they called you Cosmo,
After someone we don't know.

The Grahams told you lots of lies
About the family tree,
Like, we Montrose Grahams were
Highland Scots of great nobility.

But our Grahams came from Ireland,
To Bytown where they grew,
Nine score and ten years hence,
And now we're celebrating you.

You didn't want a birthday bash,
You didn't want a fuss,
But the Grahams never listen, so,
Too bad, you're stuck with us!

# Don't Risk Everything for a Moment of Pleasure...

*Inspired by Aesop's Fables.*

### I

A teeny weeny mousie
Spies a juicy piece of cheese,
He tiptoes round the mousetrap,
His dinner for to seize.

Snap goes the mousetrap!
Up flies the cheese!
The doggy found a cheesy treat,
And mousie got a squeeze.

### II

The weather it was windy
On the bride's most special day,
The pictures show her veil and train
Were nearly blown away.

Atop a rock she posed herself,
Her backdrop was the sea,
The camera clicked and she was gone,
A lasting memory.

### III

This cold and frosty winter's night
He thought he'd try to skate
To a hot tub, spa, and disco bar
Across the frozen lake.

He danced and soaked and bathed in mud,
And drank too many beers,
With happy thoughts he skated home,
But froze off both his ears.

## *Food Dilemmas*

Pressure diastolic, uric acid, BMI,
Eat that all-dressed pizza and you're surely gonna die.

Bacon has its nitrites, salmon's full of lead,
Pet food has no meat at all, it's made of corn instead.

Butter, cream, and eggs are now called saturated fats,
Bad for baby, bad for me, and even bad for cats.

Sugar makes you ADD and caffeine makes you quiver,
Timmy's Double-Double, guaranteed to jolt your liver.

Drugstore diet candy has no flavour or aroma,
But Easter Bunny goodies cause a diabetic coma.

Lettuce has no chlorophyll, leeks are full of grit,
Oranges are really green, and mushrooms grow in horse manure.

The fun has gone from mealtime, and of that there is no doubt,
So, eat anything you want but if it tastes good — spit it out!

## *Foot Care*

I have often wondered, goodness knows,
Why men don't wear nail polish on their toes.
The colours are gorgeous, their effect so dramatic,
And they add some pizzazz to feet monochromatic.
A "John Deere Green" could surely inspire,
Or a "Footballer Brown," or a "Harley Black Tire."

So, I asked my husband if he knows
Why men don't wear nail polish on their toes.
He thought and he stated, quite matter-of-factly,
"Because they don't want to, and that's it exactly."
Well then, what's with the white teeth, and tans, and tattoos,
Boy-Bags and earrings, Botox and hairdos?

I began to suspect that men just aren't aware
Of the paybacks of pedal extremity care.
Just remember how Fergie attracted new beaux
When her Weight Watchers diet revealed all her toes?
Men, don't leave your footsies to hide in the dust,
Enhance them with Olive, or Khaki, or Rust!

## Fountain of Youth

*From a prompt to write about a magical place.*

Our Juan Ponce de Leon, a young Spanish peon,
A soldier in Ferdinand's army,
Once had a great notion to take to the ocean,
Which, those days, was thought of as barmy.

King Ferd had foretold there were mountains of gold,
Go west, he suggested, profoundly,
Puerto Rico was found and the gold did abound,
Juan there did ensconce himself roundly.

But that Fountain of Youth, was it really the truth?
Magic waters from Lake Okeechobee,
Being ever the sleuth, with perhaps a sore tooth,
Juan fell for the sheer hyperbole.

Ponce de Leon set sail, found the place without fail,
But his dreams all were shattered in Florida.
Tales of youth were soon spun, now the spot's overrun
As the snowbirds make Florida horrider.

## Green Bin Blues

*Written after experiencing green bin recycling problems while living in a rural location.*

At the bottom of my laneway sits a shiny new green bin,
Now I need to buy a pick-up truck to fit the darn thing in,
A minor inconvenience for the latest garbage style,
Guess I'll drag it up the laneway, it's only half a mile.

Refrain:
Oh, quality time with the garbage, what better life could I choose,
I got the doesn't fit anywhere Green Bin Blues.

First, I fold the daily paper to create a funny hat,
Then I place it in the white bin, lay the garbage out on that,
Dump the white bin into the green bin, and it has liners too,
But no matter what the package, it turns to maggot stew.

Refrain:
Oh, quality time with the garbage, what better life could I choose,
I got the triple wrapped compost Green Bin Blues.

The animals here in the country, they love my new green bin,

That fancy plastic container that I store my lettuce in,

The squirrel chews on the handle, the raccoon picks at the lock,

The black bear tried to get inside by throwing it round the block.

Refrain:

Oh, quality time with the garbage, what better life could I choose,

I got the feeding the wildlife Green Bin Blues.

Carpets I take to the landfill, the light bulbs back to the store,

Paint and solvents on Tuesdays, now I'm driving a whole lot more.

Batteries go to the east end, computers they go to the west,

But stuffin' them all in a green bag is the method that I like the best.

Refrain:

Oh, quality time with the garbage, what better life could I choose,

I got the chauffeuring garbage, hole in the ozone, saving the planet, Green Bin Blues.

## *How Many Links in a Chain...*

How many times do I think of you,
How often do I say your name,
I add up our moments together,
How many links in a chain.

I want one more chance just to see your face,
And brush back the hair from your eye,
To straighten your blanket, or sing to you,
But so many days have gone by.

Sum up all the words we have spoken,
How often do I wonder why,
It seems I can never stop counting,
Yet so many years have gone by.

## I Am Not Your Granny

*A Pantoum poem has a series of quatrains with a particular repetition of lines. The first and last lines are the same.*

At least she still knew her own mind.
She did not want to sing a war song.
Their sunny lunging smiles were not warm.
"I am not your granny," she shrieked.

She did not want to sing a war song.
In her head words rollicked and tumbled.
"I am not your granny," she shrieked.
Her sputtering pleas slackened into groans.

In her head words rollicked and tumbled.
Their sunny lunging smiles were not warm.
Her sputtering pleas slackened into groans.
At least she still knew her own mind.

## *I Know Your Face*

*A poem about someone in a long-term care facility.*

Please, take me home. What is this place?
That man outside is watching me.
You're lovely dear. I know your face.
My mother's meeting me for tea.

That man outside is watching me.
Someone help me find the door,
My mother's meeting me for tea.
Now tell me what this pill is for.

Someone help me find the door.
No! I've never seen your face.
Now tell me what this pill is for.
Isn't this a lovely place?

There. He's the man who stole my purse.
You're lovely dear. I know your face.
There is NO need to call a nurse.
Just take me home. What is this place?

*I like the way you…*

- wear two wristwatches and a stopwatch too
- tell me the time over and over
- pat my back each time you circle past
- walk around when I'm washing your face
- see no need to have a bath
- don't mind getting a needle, but hate Band-Aids
- talk like a robot, and say, "You must obey. You must obey."
- always wear a hat, even in bed
- swear at yourself when you do something you shouldn't
- never pull your pants up straight
- laugh when you get the hiccoughs
- make the cat meow by doing your bad cat imitations
- throw balls for the dog backwards, over your shoulder
- say, "I hope so," instead of "yes"
- collect cash register receipts in a paper bag
- notice when I have my hair cut
- think everyone who cries is crying "'cause he misses his mother," even the dog
- refer to your brother as "the nerd"
- keep a wad of tangled tape measures in your pocket

- close all the kitchen doors that I leave open

- put garbage in the drawer

- call your favourite nurse "Red Person" because she has red hair

- bow like Bob Barker

- say "bonjour" even though you don't speak French

- pour hot sauce all over your meat

- drink a full glass of water without stopping

- put all your favourite things into the bed and then climb in on top

- never complain no matter how sick you get

- press your forehead against mine, stare into my eyes and say, "Mummy? I love you."

## *If Every Kiss Were Magic*

*Some people believe that love heals all.*

If every kiss were magic,
How could you fade away?
Our hugs and smiles and laughter,
They should have made you stay.

Nor was our love a remedy
To hold the world at bay.
Our love was all around you,
But you're not here today.

## I'm On the Outs With Brussels Sprouts

I'm on the outs with Brussels sprouts—
What recipe can save them?
Like cauliflower and cabbages,
No diner loves or craves them.

Cheap and cheerful broccoli
Is not a taste we savour,
And kidney, French, or fava beans—
All roughage, with no flavour.

Squashes make me nauseous,
So tasteless, and so bland,
And to make them more distasteful,
I must dig them out by hand.

Leave the carrots on your plate
Cause no-one's going to steal them,
But peas can please, and need no cheese,
And I don't have to peel them.

Cooking makes me weep with joy,
And sniffle in my stew,
I add a yellow onion, chopped,
And weep away. Boo hoo!

# *Integration*

*An acrostic poem uses words following the order of the alphabet (a, b, c, etc.).*

Apparently, baboons create distasteful evocations
frequenting gorilla houses.

Integration just kyboshed leisure moments,
needlessly overturning privacy.

Quarrelers raged. Screeches, then undignified vocalizations,
were X-rated, yielding zilch.

## *I Wished*

I wished that you would hold my hand
And walk along with me.

I wished that you would call my name
And sit upon my knee.

I wished that you would change yourself,
Just listen, and obey.

And then I saw that I had nearly
Wished you all away.

## Landlord Life

*This Terza Rima poem was inspired by "Acquainted with the Night," by Robert Frost.*

The hydro's off, so sorry to complain,
We have no lights, our stairway's in the dark.
I must go "out in rain — and back in rain."

Who owns that truck? I have no place to park.
Some dog has defecated by the door,
I thought she said her Great Dane didn't bark.

What's leaking? There's a puddle on the floor.
This fridge feels warm, is that a warning sign?
His garbage tags are lost, he wants some more.

The rent will be a few days late this time.
My boyfriend broke the window Friday night,
He's moving in, I hope that you don't mind.

Another guy "acquainted with the night."
But just in time the cell phone rings again,
A tenant with an urgent plumbing plight,

And once again I hear that sweet refrain,
My toilet's plugged, so sorry to complain!

# Listen! O Listen! (Gaelic is Éist! O Éist!)

*A toast to Jessie Norma McArthur Norman on the occasion of her 100th birthday, in Kincardine, Ontario.*

Listen! O Listen! the Clan members cry.
McArthurs assemble, a birthday is nigh.
So, bung out your sporrans ye Lassies and Lads,
And brush off your kilties, there's cake to be had!

Call Duncan and Donald, the Dougals and Dans,
Archibald, Angus, Amelias and Anns!
Kincardine, Kilmartin, Kilmichael Glassary,
Argyllshire, Oban, Loch Fyne, Inverary.

Come teachers and preachers and farmers and kin,
The big celebration's about to begin.
Ten decades she's charmed us (that's four score and twenty),
For birthday experience Jessie's had plenty.

Now light up the cake for the one we admire,
But please clear the exits in case there's a fire.
To our own Jessie Norma we raise a wee dram,
And drink to the health of the head of the clan.

## *Medical Advances*

When I swelled up and itched all over and gained too much
weight,
The obstetrician said I was anxious.
Take these pills and stay away from chocolate.
Although you were born three weeks late, he said you were fine.

The pediatrician said all babies cry,
That you would eat when you got hungry, and sleep when you
were tired.
All toddlers fall down he said.
He gripped the doorknob while I talked.

The day you stopped breathing the ER doctor said you probably
choked, or had a fever.
He looked closely for hidden bruises and made a note in your file.
When you turned blue again and again, he asked me how long my
pregnancy was.
He recommended tests.

The radiologist said to bring you back when I could keep you still.

The internist said your incontinence was just attention-seeking.

He slapped you and told you to stop.

He said I let you get away with things.

The psychologist said you needed behaviour modification.

Give him Smarties when he behaves and a cold bath when he does not.

I charted our battle on the fridge.

We both lost.

The psychiatrist asked me if I loved you.

Did I really want to be a mother? Was my marriage happy?

He suggested therapy,

For me.

The neurologist watched you run.

"Does he sleep well? Does he fall?" He tapped your knees and did a scan.

"I'm so sorry," he said. "He's autistic and has a seizure disorder."

I said, "That's the best news I've ever had."

## Mismatched

*A 108-word Postcard Story... that is, a story small enough to fit on a postcard.*

She looked over the forks in the cutlery drawer. She considered giving him the mismatched one. After all, he wouldn't notice, would he? And even if he did notice, he wouldn't care. To him, a fork was a means to an end, something used to convey food to the mouth. And, should the fork not appear in the usual place, he would simply use his fingers.

She chose the matching fork. She still cared about the niceties of daily life. And where would they be if neither of them cared? She should be glad he used a fork at all. She had already given up on the napkins.

## Murderin' Minnie

Now Murderin' Minnie, the merciless cat
Was hunting for mousies so juicy and fat,
She watched and she watched till her dinner she spied,
And the mouse was so shocked that he plain up and died.

She began at the front with the ears, eyes and nose,
Then the skull and the neck, and she nibbled some toes,
But Murderin' Minnie was quite mathematical,
She halted her feast when she got to the clavicle.

Mouse heads are so crunchy with much in their favour,
But back ends of mice are quite lacking in flavour.
So, when she had eaten the head and two feet,
She felt that her dinner was quite incomplete.

Still feeling peckish and wanting another,
She went on the hunt for a sister, or brother,
For whole mice will do for the snakes and the crows,
But two heads are better, as every cat knows.

## My Ancestry

*Can be sung to the traditional tune "Spanish Ladies." The Canadian version begins, "We'll rant and we'll roar like true Newfoundlanders."*

There's Porter and Dollin, then Quick, White and Fleming,
MacPherson and Westley, McCulloch, McPhee,
McLarty, McAmmond, McArthur, McCallum,
The Grahams and the Taylors, the Whites and Scobies.

The McArthur-McCallums came down from the Highlands,
With Campbells, McLartys, and ten more in tow.
They stopped at Lake Huron and built some nice farms there,
And gave three Gaelic parsons to Ontario.

McCulloch from Scotland, he landed in Whitby,
And too late he married a girl named McPhee,
Had twin boys too quickly, then parents both vanished,
One to the Gold Rush and one—don't ask me.

The Monaghan Grahams came directly to Bytown,
They farmed and sold lumber all up the Valley,
The men died too early, the families all scattered,
But one lived just long enough to produce me.

Now Benjamin Franklin convinced Mr. Westley
To move to the US from Norfolk County,
He soon crossed the border ahead of the Patriots,
And joined all the Scots in nearby Glengarry.

It seems all my ancestors came from the same place,
England and Ireland and Scotland, that's all,
I hope they weren't cousins, or brothers and sisters…
Did I mention I'm 2.3 percent Neanderthal?

## My Love is Not a Red Rose

*Inspired by the Robbie Burns poem," My Love is Like a Red, Red Rose."*

Can my love make you happier,
Or drive away your tears?
And is your life more beautiful
Because I hold you dear?

Or would you soar far higher
If I were to let you go?
And would you sing less sweetly
If I did not love you so?

My love cannot protect you
From the ravages of time,
You are not safe from sadness
Just because I made you mine.

My love is not a red rose,
More like a climbing vine,
Which binds us both together,
And thus, our lives confine.

## My Luv 4 U

*Inspired by talking with some local tattoo artists.*

So I could prove my LUV 4 U,
I got myself a big tattoo.
Cuz you and I will never part,
I had your face inked near my heart.

Our luv is wider than the sky,
Higher than stars on the 4th of July.
My sincereness is unbending,
Our true luv is never-ending.

Oh, how I luv your Chinese signs,
Your python arms, your zipper spine,
The way your neck says TAKE A BITE,
The way your feet say LEFT and RITE.

Your knuckles reading HATE and LOVE,
Green lizard skin for sleeve and glove,
Pope John 23$^{rd}$ smiles from your hip,
And it says PEACE inside your lip.

But if our love should ever falter,
I could get my tattoos altered,
Fix the J in I LOVE JAKE
To say instead that I LOVE CAKE.

I could get my poems changed,
Have your portrait rearranged,
A smiling skull deletes your face,
My words of love re-inked as lace.

## No Trouble Here

You are different now. Your laugh has gone cool, you are mild and firm and still.
Your once sharp wit, now over-honed, seems cutting and snide.

No longer modest, you are now just prim, and your sincerity is practiced and trite.
I sense you have a time and a place reserved for me. We must paint within the lines now.

Your inner life is boxed and stored away. Your thoughts are tidy, neat and clean.
You have sorted and filed, tossed away the mismatched, and muted the colours.

You guide our conversation, keeping me safe from myself. I must not stray.
When I swing too close, you counter with well-scrubbed thoughts.

You hold fast, secure in the recitation of names, dates and events,
While I try to derail you by asking how and why.

Your determined goodness is smothering and shuts me out. You show a brave face, but I sense your defeat.

But never mind. I will continue to smile and keep to your well-worn paths.
We want no trouble here.

## Pup in da Hood

*For Scooter, a chihuahua and terrier mix, aka Scoot-Dog.*

It's a busy day for me,
Gotta pee on every tree,
Have a nap on someone's knee,
I'm a pup in da hood.

Yo' doorman, lemme out,
I be cruising all about,
Get some poop upon my snout,
I'm a pup in da hood.

In the yard I got my posse,
Cats and squirrels being saucy,
It's a good thing I'm so bossy,
I'm a pup in da hood.

Hey, I'm barking can't you hear?
Bring my kibble over here,
Now I'm gonna lick my rear,
I'm a pup in da hood.

Got some classy winter boots
And a velvet Santa suit,
I'm so ugly that I'm cute,
I'm a pup in da hood.

Hardly ever have to fight
'Cause I treat my people right,
Let them sleep with me at night,
I'm a pup in da hood.

Yo, the ladies call me Scooter,
In my crib I am a shooter,
Wazzup with that word "neuter"?
No more pups in the hood!

## *Shearing Sheep at Forest Row*

The helpers don their woolen gear and gather round the pen,
To watch some nervous sheep get shorn, because it's spring again.
The shearer's got his kilt on, the bleating's underway,
In spite of the snow at Forest Row, today is shearing day.

The sheep are getting nervous and some try to climb the fence,
They don't recall last spring at all, but sheep can be so dense.
Perhaps they will be killed and turned to mutton, chops, or racks,
But no! We want to shave their wool off and then wear it on our
backs!

They stick their heads in corners and in one another's rears,
"I'm not here," they're thinking, as they try to dodge the shears.
But are sheep really thinking, we wonder as we stare,
Can't they see how cool they'll be some day when summer's
here?

When sheep sit back with legs askew they have a thoughtful look,
Could it be they're smart enough to knit, or read a book?
But no, it seems that new-shorn sheep no longer know each other,
Are you my dad, my son, my twin? If you're a girl, my mother?

Once the sheep are naked, they get dragged across the floor

Like United Airlines passengers, but worth a little more.

Their hooves are trimmed, the boo-boos dressed, their fleece is rolled and gone,

Then out they go into the snow, to pray for summer sun.


Look out! A sheep can take you for a sudden bareback ride,

And if you're facing backwards, it's much more undignified.

Their bells on leather collars sag around their scrawny necks,

They flick their tails and skip around, and grumble, "What the feck"?

## Sorting Through Clothes on a Summer Evening

*...with apologies to Robert Frost, "Stopping by Woods on a Snowy Evening."*

Whose pants these are I think I know,
The waistband is a way too low;
The crotch is short both front and rear,
Who knew how much my ass would grow.

My husband must have thought it queer
To see me wear a dress so sheer,
I knew it was a big mistake
Just as the blind man turned to cheer.

My cowgirl vest of rattlesnake,
A poncho made of leather, fake,
The rhinestone sweater plunging deep,
I need to give my head a shake.

And in the winter dark and deep
A ten-foot scarf I'll purchase, cheap,
And high-heeled boots to make me weep,
And high-heeled boots to make me weep.

## Spring!

Robins bouncing,
Kittens pouncing,
Crows announcing
Spring!

Maples sapping,
Beavers slapping,
Geese are crapping,
Spring.

Marsh hawk soaring,
Chainsaws roaring,
Golfers "fore-ing,"
Spring.

Froggies creaking,
Pond is reeking,
Basement leaking,
Spring.

Pollen flyin',
Eyes are cryin',
Dandelion,
Spring.

Seeds are sprouting,
Creek is trouting,
Skiers pouting,
Spring.

Tent unpacking,
Bugs attacking,
Campers whacking,
Spring.

Raindrops pelting,
Dog doo melting,
Songbirds belting
Spring!

Lawn mower gagging,

Eavestrough sagging,

Asses dragging,

Spring.


Tulips flopping,

Blossoms dropping,

Rainfall stopping...

　　Bummer. It's summer.

## Spring Cleaning

I used to spend the springtime with a rag on bended knee,
But I deserved more modern ways to clean efficiently.
So I got a cyclone vacuum just to pick up all the dirt,
It sucked the sheets right off the bed and stole my husband's shirt.

Now window washing isn't always what I love to do,
With cluster flies and splotches of assorted birdie poo.
The pressure washer worked a charm to blast off all the sludge,
But now I have to paint again, I'm once again a drudge.

I hauled out all my summer clothes and dumped them on the floor,
They're even smaller this year than they were the year before.
Good bye to halter tops and thongs and shrunken double knits
My bathing suit has lost its stretch, at least my hat still fits.

The Hindu goddess Kali represents the perfect wife,
She waves her six appendages and organizes life.
My head is in the oven now, one arm is in the loo,
Another sorts the laundry out, I need more arms, don't you?

## Square Dancing In the ER

You're not dying, take a chair,
By Thursday night we should be there.
Don't have drinks, or stuff to eat,
No bathroom visits, keep your seat.

Near-death people, line up here,
Shoulders back and speak real clear.
Those who writhe about and cry,
Back of the line – you're gonna die.

When slumping over with palpitations,
Shout "cardiopulmonary resuscitation!"
But if you faint and hit the floor,
And smash your face, you really score.

The cyanotic blue-faced boy
Can skip the front desk hoi polloi,
Another way to get a pass,
Just have a seizure on broken glass.

Weeping mothers – so neurotic
Fussing when their child's psychotic.
To give yourself a fighting chance,
Take your trip by ambulance.

Be unconscious, try to bleed,
Crushing chest pain's what you need.
But those who feel their time has come,
Here's the number for 911.

## The Dreamer and the Warrior

The Dreamer, always making plans,
The luxury of time,
Hopes and wishes thin as air,
That once were yours and mine.

The Warrior can make no plans
And lives from day to day,
His path to truth is short and straight,
No dreaming on the way.

## The Little Boys

*Inspired by a Canadian photograph called, "Wait for Me Daddy," of a small boy in New Westminster, British Columbia, who leaves his mother to run alongside soldiers marching off to war.*

The little boys, they like to march
Behind the flag and drums,
They step in time and thump their boots
And swing their tiny guns.

Their fathers march before them
In a never-ending line,
They call out, "Come and join the men
And leave the girls behind."

Their mothers cannot hold them back,
The beat of war is strong,
They wave and smile and blow a kiss,
And then their boys are gone.

The little boys, they like to march
Behind the flag and drums,
They step in time and thump their boots
And swing their tiny guns.

## The Little Box

There's a little box inside me
Up on my highest shelf,
A little box of memories
I keep just for myself.

No one else can look inside,
I have the only key,
To the little box wherein I save
The life of you and me.

Treasured cherished moments,
A life that now is gone,
Our smiles and fears, our laughs and tears,
And days we struggled on.

The little box inside me
Holds the life that we once knew,
A funny hat, a crooked smile,
A "Mummy, I love you."

### *The Modest Writer*

*Written on the occasion of the 80ʰ birthday of Sybil McDonnell.*

A talented writer named Sybil,
Wrote stories both witty and ribald,
Eschewing all fame
And pecuniary gain,
She quibbled, "My scribble is drivel."

## The Owl and the Pussycat

*A variant of a Glosa poem, based on the poem, "The Owl and the Pussycat," by Edward Lear, with the beginning of each stanza written by Lear, followed by my expanded version. Lear's words are bolded and in quotation marks.*

**"The Owl and the Pussycat went to sea**
**In a beautiful pea green boat,**
**They took some honey, and plenty of money**
**Wrapped up in a five-pound note."**

### Glosa Version

**"The Owl and the Pussycat went to sea"**
In search of a cool wedding venue,
'O Pussy my love, by the stars above,
Let's have mince and sliced quince on the menu,
The menu,
The menu,
Let's have mince and sliced quince on the menu.'

*"In a beautiful pea-green boat,"* they sailed,

To a land where the Bong tree grew,

The Owl sang to Pussy, 'Please marry me.'

And the Pussy responded, 'Yes mew,

Oh mew,

Yes mew.'

And the Pussy responded, 'Yes, mew!'


*"They took some honey, and plenty of money"*

And attracted a pig with a ring,

They offered a shilling, but was the pig willing?

"How much do you want for that bling,

That bling,

That bling,

How much do you want for that bling?"

*"Wrapped up in a five-pound note"* there remained
The ring and a runcible spoon,
They hired a preacher, a foul barnyard creature,
And got hitched by the light of the moon,
The moon,
The moon,
And got hitched by the light of the moon.

## The Romantic Tale of Pigoletto and Porcina

Poor Pigoletto lived alone, with neither a dad nor mum,
No friend to share a squeal with, or wallow in the sun,
"I guess I was an only child," he pondered quizzically,
"I thought I had some litter mates, but no one's left but me."

Porcina lived behind the fence, a porky classic beauty,
Round and pink and full of fat, a real hot patootie.
"Oink." said she. "Did I just hear a grunt behind the gate?"
"I'm here." he squealed. My dream's come true. I think I found a mate."

Pigoletto and Porcina passed many a blissful day,
And the farmer sure was happy when some piglets came their way.
Dear Hammy was the juiciest, so easy to digest,
Porketta was the spicy one, but Liverwurst was best!

## *Waiting*

Where are you?
Everything is ready.
Why are you late, so late?
Maybe I should call to remind you.

I'll just read a bit.
No need to be concerned.
Perhaps the roads are bad.
I'm sure you'll have a story to tell.

I suppose you could be lost,
But you did ask me for directions.
Or are you hurt?
Or maybe you just can't be bothered to call.

When you arrive, I'll act unconcerned,
Or maybe I'll be stern.
Wasn't this meeting all your idea?
Why did I take such trouble to prepare?

Fine. It seems you are not coming.
I'm starting without you.
Unless you're in the hospital or worse,
Don't even bother calling.

That's it! I'm putting this food away,
And no more looking down the lane.
I don't really care what happened.
Oh, why don't you just call?

Okay. I got your message,
You're sorry. You're embarrassed.
You thought it was Thursday.
Yes. I'll be home tomorrow.

## The Wake-up Cats

*Not doggerel, but "catterel."*

Hello, tickle-whisker cat
On my stomach, you're too fat.
Go and gallop down the hall,
Like you did when you were small.

Can't you find a chair to claw,
A plate to lick, toothbrush to gnaw?
There's a lamp about to tip,
Glass of water, have a sip.

Where's your crazy sister kitten?
Oh, she's helping with my knittin'.
Soon she'll be a grown-up cat,
And just like you, she'll be too fat!

## *Where Did You Go?*

*The Terza Rima is a three-line chain poem, a style first used by Dante Alighieri. The traditional version has a rhyme scheme of aba bcb cdc, and so on, and ends with a rhyming couplet.*

You were too fast
I knew somehow you'd slip away,
It couldn't last.

I tried so hard to make you stay.
I was unsure,
And why you left I couldn't say.

Would I endure?
You called me but it was too late,
Who could be sure.

I held you but you couldn't wait,
Was I too slow?
Again, goodbye, it was our fate.

Where did you go?
I'll never know.

*Without the encouragement of my weekly writing group, led by Beth Beasley, this book never would have happened. Thank you for laughing and crying in all the right places. And thanks to Terri for her technical advice, and Editor Laurie for helping me get it on the page. And to Jack, thank you for listening.*

Made in the USA
Middletown, DE
14 May 2019